Undertaken
With Love

A Home Funeral Guide for Families and Community Care Groups

By Holly Stevens

Revised 2016 by Donna Belk

About the National Home Funeral Alliance (NHFA)

www.homefuneralalliance.org

The NHFA, an all-volunteer 503(c)(3) non-profit, has the mission to educate the public about their choices and provide clear information about all things relating to home funerals.

We empower families to care for their own dead by providing educational opportunities and connections to resources that promote environmentally sound and culturally nurturing death practices. We share information about home funerals, including directories for where to find home funeral guides, home funeral education programs, home-funeral-friendly funeral directors, celebrants and clergy, and groups who will help families when needed.

Created in 2010, our members come from all over the world. Many of us are home funeral guides who also identify as licensed funeral directors, ordained ministers, educators, body workers, licensed social workers, registered nurses, therapists and counselors, directors of nonprofits, attorneys and physicians. Anyone can become a member of the NHFA, participate on committees, access the Member Resources section on the website, and request mentorship.

NATIONAL HOME FUNERAL ALLIANCE
11014 19th Ave SE, Ste #8, PMB #155
Everett, WA 98208

Table of Contents

The images in this book are a combination of "skeleton leaves" purchased from image stock services, and the illustrations of Ann Manning (used with permission, © 2007 Jack Manning and Friends). Ann Manning was a remarkable artist and her family provided her with a home funeral. Ann's deeply touching home funeral is described in detail by her husband in a free PDF manuscript. Visit www.jackmanningllc.com/no_grey_suits to download.

©2016 Donna Belk
Layout and design: Donna Belk

ISBN-13: 978-1533638724

ISBN-10: 1533638721

Printed in the United States of America

Acknowledgments

Contributing Writers: Donna Belk, Margalo Eden, Gere B. Fulton, Wendy Lyons, Joyce Mitchell, Holly Stevens, Lee Webster, Kateyanne Unullisi.

Artwork: Ann Manning, courtesy of Jack Manning & Friends

Nested 2 by Ann Manning

Personal Note from the Editor

By Donna Belk

The credit for this book goes to Holly Stevens, now deceased, who knew she was terminally ill and wanted to leave a legacy for others in the form of this book. She originated the idea for this manual and saw it to publication, She worked, even in her illness, to produce *Undertaken With Love* because she so believed in the healing power of home funerals.

When she was very close to death, the book was finished, and she asked me to take over the distribution and future revisions of *Undertaken With Love*. It is an honor to help her legacy continue by updating this publication, and giving it over to the National Home Funeral Alliance (NHFA) to carry it forward. The book is very much in alignment with the mission of the NHFA: to educate families about their right to home funerals and provide them with information and resources to make that a possibility.

In loving memory of Holly Stevens, whose heart and words weave this book together.

Foreword

By Lee Webster, President, National Home Funeral Alliance

Throughout this book, you'll find images of leaves, denuded of the organic matter that once made up the flesh of the living, breathing leaf of the Quaking Aspen tree. It's no accident that this symbol found its way into a book about caring for our own dead.

Homer described "the aspen's glancing leaves" as singularly formed to flutter with the slightest breath of wind. These trees are considered to be the largest living organism on Earth, and some the oldest as well. They are the first to self-propagate after wildfires, enduring an amazing array of adverse soil and sun conditions, growing nearly everywhere in the US.

Aspen trees provide shade all summer with their spreading canopy, and delight and calm us with their musical rustling sounds even on still evenings. They shed stunning yellow leaves in fall, the perfect counterpoint to the reds and oranges of autumn. And once their leaves have lost their rich covering, their ribs, their netted veins and veinlets, their very shape stays constant, skeletons strong yet delicate as the air.

Our bodies, once filled with vitality, once responding to whatever wind blew by, eventually swell and empty of breath for the last time. Whatever we have weathered in our lifetime, how many times we have sprung back from adversity, reinvented ourselves, learned to love and live and join in the chorus of many, we will each, one day, fall.

Whether in family or larger community, care of our dead at home is an intimate, transformative experience. We at once defend against the onerous passing of time with its threat of decay and disorder by bathing and touching for the last time, while we simultaneously experience the fleeting beauty that our loved ones often reveal to us in their last hours.

With all the artifice and struggle and mortal maintenance stripped away, we may yet discover the bone-deep strength that lay beneath us all that time, silently holding us and the deceased up. Home funeral families don't fear what they will find when nature marches on after death: they witness it, care for it, make peace with it, and find meaning in it.

This book provides a sturdy framework for caring for the dead. It is our fervent hope that the tools and techniques you learn here will provide the practical, logistical, and spiritual support you need so that you may know the joys and sorrows, in equal measure, of caring for a loved one at home after death.

And don't forget: none of us falls from that tree alone, though we may fall at different times. Home funerals are about building and participating in community as well as individual freedom to choose a personal after-death path. Reach out, cultivate partners, and create after-death practices and experiences that resonate with strength, compassion, and respect. One leaf at a time.

Introduction

By Holly Stevens

When Nellie Hickerson, of Randleman, NC, died in early 2008, she went to the grave in the same manner that she had lived her final years—lovingly tended by her children C.L. Hickerson and Suzanne Poorman on the family's 80-acre rural homestead.

For three days, Nellie's body lay in her bedroom, cooled by dry ice and the ice bottles that grandson Matthew Poorman had stashed ahead of time in the freezer. Captured earlier on a CD, Nellie's voice sang out now and then in a hauntingly ethereal Southern twang: "I once was lost, but now am found, was blind, but now I see."

A third sibling drove down from Wilton, NH, for the Friday burial in the homestead graveyard where C.L. had previously reinterred his father's remains. An unlined cedar casket made by a neighbor waited nearby. Meanwhile, friends and church members prepared meals, took pictures and brought shovels. Someone even thought to stash tampers and a rake for finishing the site afterward.

In the end, Nellie was laid to rest beside her husband on the only tract of land she'd ever known intimately, her grave adorned with the wildflowers and herbs she'd admired all her life.

If this story sounds fanciful, despite the fact that it really happened, it is only because we've grown so accustomed in the past century to handing over the care of our own dead to institutional caregivers. There is nothing wrong with hiring professional funeral providers, of course. But in recent years, more families like the Hickersons have opted to care for their own loved ones all the way to final disposition.

In all but a handful of states, a family may serve as its own funeral director in caring for its dead until burial or cremation. Planning ahead is a must and it does require attention to a few regulations and a willingness to be something of a pioneer in communicating your intentions to those who will be involved. But many who have chosen this route will tell you that they found it to be enormously healing and satisfying. Many crematories and cemeteries have policies that preclude accepting delivery of the body by the family, so finding a crematory operator or cemetery sexton who will honor your desire to do the bulk of the work is crucial. Gaining clarity around the details, and making connections when planning ahead will serve you well when the time comes to implement your plan.

What this book is about

This book is written for the individual, a family, or community care groups. The second half of the book is a study guide to help form and maintain a community care group in your area.

Community care groups are made up of people who work together to provide information, training and assistance to people who want to learn about home funerals. While a motivated family can independently acquire the legal knowledge and practical skills to arrange a home funeral, the process is eased considerably when a group assists. Often, that support might come in the form of a faith-based community care group that embraces home funerals as a natural extension of its work in bereavement care. In other cases, an entirely secular group might evolve from a circle of close friends or neighbors or a hospice support group. Or families that are planning to have a home funeral can come together to learn and help each other with their funerals.

We've created this book to help individual families and community care groups who opt to care for their own loved ones from the moment of death until burial or cremation. The book's aims are to:
- provide step-by-step instructions for how to start a community-based home funeral community care group;
- suggest a continuum of options in funerals from entirely institutional models to entirely home-centered models;
- teach the skills involved in handling, preparing, cooling, laying out and transporting the dead to the cemetery or crematory;
- convey the necessity of researching and grasping local and state laws that relate to home funerals and how to acquire the necessary knowledge; and
- offer ideas for sustaining the home funeral care group.

Whether used in a congregational or a secular setting, *Undertaken With Love* will provide the basic knowledge and skills to launch a home funeral support system in your community.

In most of the United States, a family may care for its own dead until burial or cremation without involving licensed funeral professionals. It does require a willingness to be something of a pioneer in today's hands-off society, but those who have chosen to reclaim this historical tradition confirm that the process is enormously healing and meaningful.

The home funeral movement has grown since the original publication of this book, and there are now people available who are doing this work in different communities. You can find a listing of the people offering services in the different areas by visiting the National Home Funeral Alliance website at homefuneralalliance.org. There you will find a directory of practitioners in the "Get Assistance" section. You can contact home funeral guides, celebrants, end-of-life transition guides and others for any part that you or your group might want help with. You can do all of the work involved with a home funeral by yourself, or do some of it yourself and contact others for help with other aspects, including a funeral director. There is no right or wrong way that a home or family-directed funeral should be done. The best way is the way that serves the individual family members, and then the larger community.

While a motivated family can independently acquire the legal knowledge and practical skills to arrange a home funeral, the process is eased considerably when a group assists. That's why we've created *Undertaken With Love*: to help faith-based and secular groups support families that want to continue caring for their loved ones all the way to the grave or crematory.

If you are working in a group, use the Study Guide section of the book and meet for weekly or monthly self-training sessions. This book will teach you:
- how to start a home funeral care group;
- how to research state laws and identify your legal rights and responsibilities;
- how to handle, bathe and transport the deceased; and
- how to sustain an effective home funeral care group.

One challenge we faced in writing the book was reaching agreement on what to call this work. Some prefer the moniker "family-directed funeral" to differentiate it from a funeral directed by licensed funeral directors. Others use "home death care," "natural funeral," family-centered death care" or other combinations. After much give and take, we settled on *home funeral* as our primary term for the work and *home funeral care group* to denote the group that assists the family. They are not perfect descriptors. The word "funeral" carries multiple meanings—from the ceremony, to the procession to the grave, to the actual committal, to the entire process. Also, not all home funerals will occur in the home; some faith communities shelter the body, for instance. But the term "home funeral" seems to be gaining favor in most of the literature, perhaps because it falls more gently on the ear than its "death care" counterparts, and it is simple. For clarity, we are using the definition provided by the National Home Funeral Alliance:

> A home funeral happens when a loved one is cared for at home or in a sacred space after death, giving family and friends time to prepare the body, file legal paperwork, and gather and grieve in private. Home funerals can be held at the family home or not. Some nursing homes, church community care groups and funeral homes may allow the family to care for the deceased after death. The emphasis is on minimal, non-inva-

sive, and environmentally friendly care of the body. Support and assistance to carry out after-death care may come from home funeral educators or guides, but their goal is to facilitate maximum involvement of the family in charge of the funeral process, and their social network.

The actual tasks carried out by the home funeral care group will vary according to its aims.

One home funeral care group might be motivated most of all by the desire to embrace equality at life's end by purchasing inexpensive caskets in bulk and negotiating reduced rates for an immediate burial or cremation through a local funeral provider. Another home funeral care group might be drawn especially to natural practices focusing on gentle, nonchemical care of the body in a home setting followed by burial in a biodegradable casket in a natural, or green, cemetery, which eschews vaults that would inhibit the process of "returning to the earth."

Certainly a faith-based funeral care group would want to infuse its practices with its religious rituals, language and values, while a secular funeral care group might strive to avoid religious overtones that could be a hindrance to some members' participation. In writing this book, we tried to be inclusive of this diversity.

At the end of this book we have included a study guide for those who would like a more organized approach to this material. The guide offers suggested exercises that might work in some settings but not others, and we've taken care not to be prescriptive or to assume a particular orientation. We encourage you to discard any suggestions that don't fit easily with your group's culture or practices and to incorporate your own customs at every opportunity.

Home funerals are not for everyone. Certainly they are departures from the institutional manner in which Americans have arranged for death care since the early 20th century. Undoubtedly home funerals require more involvement from the family, though the support of a group can greatly ease the load. Occasionally circumstances will make a home funeral impractical, but most who have experienced home funerals share that the process was enormously healing, enabling them to participate creatively in honoring the one who died in ways that commercial funeral homes and crematories cannot replicate.

We are delighted that you are embarking on this road of discovery.

Home Funeral Timeline

By Lee Webster, President, National Home Funeral Alliance

Avoid feeling overwhelmed about having a home funeral by adopting an educated, well-organized approach to meeting the challenges one step at time. You may discover additional items that have meaning or are necessary where you live, but we hope that the timeline below will give you a solid framework to begin with.

Do some sleuthing
- Find out if your state requires a funeral director
- Learn what the requirements are for cooling and time limits

Make the plans known
- Complete advance directives
- Write an obituary
- Plan ceremony
- Figure out who you'll need to help you, and make plans with them

Go shopping
- Choose burial or cremation
- Make or purchase shroud or casket
- Gather home supplies

At death
- Contact appropriate authorities
- Contact helpers
- Conduct body care, dress and casket
- Inform community

Initiate Paperwork
- Obtain death certificate signatures
- Complete demographic section
- File and obtain transport permit

Hold vigil
- Invite friends and family, co-workers, congregants
- Decorate the space
- Arrange for food
- Invite participation

Scheduling
- Call the cemetery or crematory to schedule disposition
- Set a date for memorial
- Finalize ceremony

Finalize paperwork
- File completed cremation or burial paperwork
- Obtain certified copies of the death certificate

Tend to legal and financial matters
- Process the will
- Sell or distribute possessions
- File with Social Security
- File with military if appropriate
- Pay bills

Feel complete and know that you did the best you could

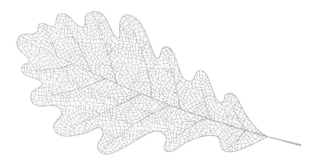

Chapter 1

Then and Now: A history of home funerals

By Donna Belk, Margalo Eden, Wendy Lyons and Holly Stevens

If you visit a funeral home today, you're apt to find a general price list that includes embalming and a sealed metal casket in its description of a "traditional" arrangement. But for most of America's history, the traditional funeral was a far more simple and affordable affair.

Many of our grandparents knew exactly what to do when a death occurred, and friends, neighbors and faith communities rallied to help. Often, at least one woman in the community possessed specialized knowledge in the laying out of the dead. Just as a midwife was called upon to assist with a birth, this "shrouding woman" could be called upon to assist following a death, and would organize the women in the cleaning and dressing of the body. Historically in America, after-death care was considered the exclusive duty of women. Meanwhile, the men built the casket, dug the grave and transported the body.

The Civil War marked the beginning of an historic transition in the way Americans would care for their dead for generations to come. When soldiers died in combat, they were typically buried in the battlefield. But families that could afford the expense often had the government transport their dead home for burial. As the number of dead increased—along with the challenges of locating and transporting decomposing corpses from battlefields, hospitals, etc.—a lucrative market for new "embalming surgeons" emerged. Contracted by the government or working independently, they performed arterial embalming to slow decomposition and better enable transportation over long distances. These embalmers were the forerunners of the modern-day funeral director.

Little by little, caring for our dead went from being an act of love freely carried out by families and communities to a trade that allows for little—if any—hands-on family involvement. And it's been that way for decades.

Reclaiming Our Past

After-death care in America is once again in a transition of historic proportions. Lisa Carlson's trailblazing book "Caring for the Dead: Your Final Act of Love," which was first published in 1987, inspired many families to rethink how to approach burial and cremation. Today, the National Home Funeral Alliance joins the Funeral Consumers Alliance in educating and empowering individuals, families, spiritual communities and consumers about their right to care for their own dead. Modern-day pioneers in family-led home funerals, including Nancy Jewel Poer, Lisa Carlson, Jerrigrace Lyons, Beth Knox, Char Barrett, Lee Webster, Donna Belk and many more, have contributed to our understanding of the practical skills involved in caring for our dead.

Likewise, those who have participated in home funerals confirm their healing benefits. Many have graciously invited the public to bear witness through photos, videos and newspaper stories so that others are inspired to follow in their footsteps. With each passing year more people choose to reconnect with this sacred tradition and welcome the funeral back into the intimacy of the home.

Although family-directed home funerals take more effort to arrange and carry out, many families feel they are more meaningful and healing than those arranged for them by a funeral director. A home funeral can help people gently integrate the death into their lives.

When the body remains at home for a few days, family and friends lovingly attend to it and remain connected to the process, their deceased loved one and each other.

A home funeral offers mourners a sense of control and helps them feel useful. It also enables families to create the ambience, to decide how the body is to be treated, to choose—without pressure—how to facilitate the most meaningful gathering for their loved one's farewell.

A home funeral does require organization and determination. Even mundane tasks, such as filing state and local forms, while not difficult to perform, may seem daunting to those deep in grief. For this reason it is important to plan ahead when possible and gather family members and friends who are willing and able to take on various responsibilities. An ongoing home funeral community care group can offer acquired wisdom and consistency to ease the process.

A home funeral can be much less costly as well. When a community comes together to provide this loving service, there are no facility fees, no fees for storing the body, no fees for transportation, flower arranging or cosmetology. Coffins or alternative containers may be crafted and decorated instead of purchased. An urn for cremated remains can be fashioned, or a simple, inexpensive container can be bought and beautifully decorated by caring hands. A family may handle all the arrangements or seek limited assistance from a funeral director for certain tasks.

Ultimately there is no one right way to hold a funeral. Every family is unique, and there are many options available to reflect that individuality. The family-directed home funeral offers a final, loving, hands-on opportunity to honor our dead and send them on their way—in their home, surrounded by the people who love them.

Chapter 2

Finding the Law: Are home funerals legal?

By Gere B. Fulton and Joyce Mitchell
Updated by Lee Webster 2016

Home funerals are legal in every state. Families can bring or keep a loved one home, bathe and prepare the body for visits, hold a home vigil, and host a ceremony, if desired. Community care groups can support the family in the home or in another private setting, including churches.

There are often state and local legal requirements that need to be addressed, and they are different in each state. It's important to understand which laws and local ordinances pertain to families, and which are only for professionals, in the form of both laws and regulations. In most states, families can file paperwork and transport with the appropriate permits, managing the finer details themselves. In some states, funeral directors are legally required to perform certain duties. Be assured that mandatory hiring of a funeral director does not preclude home vigils or a satisfying community and family-directed experience.

Community care groups and families are wise to learn the prevailing laws in their state and stay abreast of any changes in order to protect the family and safeguard the team should any challenges be issued. Understanding what families and care teams can and cannot do legally is the cornerstone on which your work is built.

Since 1984, the Federal Trade Commission (FTC) has regulated funeral industry practices with what has been termed "the Funeral Rule," 16 CFR (Code of Federal Regulations) Part 453. Federal law does not govern funerals carried out by individuals. However, these regulations do apply to anyone who provides both after-death goods and services for remuneration. If your care group charges for assisting families and sells any funerary item of any kind, you are subject to the Funeral Rule. For a detailed description of permissible home funeral activities for guides and care teams acceptable to the FTC, see "Essentials for Practicing Home Funeral Guides."

Where to Start

There are several ways to research the law and procedures for caring for your own dead.

Contact the National Home Funeral Alliance (www.homefuneralalliance.org)
The NHFA provides links to state laws and regulations. You will also find directories of home funeral guides, community care groups, and more to help with forming your group and to get answers if you have questions.

Contact a local Funeral Consumer Alliance (FCA) affiliate (www.funerals.org)
The FCA is a consumer organization that may have an affiliate in your area. Go to the website of the national organization, and click on the link "Find a Local FCA" at the top of the page. If there is an affiliate serving your area, they may already have compiled state and local legal information.

Conduct an online search
Type the name of your state followed by the word *funeral laws, regulations, statutes, code* or *rules* into your browser to get the quickest path to the laws you are seeking. For example: *South Carolina funeral regulations*. You can also go to the general state laws page for your state where you can use the search function to refine your search. Enter the words *funeral, burial, dead bodies* or *death certificate*. You should also perform this search on the website of the state agency that grants professional licenses and be sure to include a search of state health regulations and provisions.

Visit government offices
Go to your county or local health department, and ask for a copy of the procedures to be followed when a family wishes to act as its own funeral director. If you have been successful in finding the law online, bring a copy of the exact statute that grants you the right to file a death certificate. You may need to leave that copy for the worker to analyze. While this may be time consuming and may result in some interesting reactions from ill-informed or uninformed employees, it will give you some idea of procedural problems that might confront a grieving family member. It will also give you the opportunity to begin the educational process that is often needed.

If your local health department is unwilling or unable to provide this information, seek an answer from your state health department. Ask the clerk at the local department for the name, address and telephone number of the head of the appropriate division at the state department. Make a telephone call, or set up an appointment. If not terribly inconvenient, the latter is preferable. The person at the state level should be able to provide you with copies of the relevant statutes and regulations and tell you the procedures to be followed.

Another place to turn to is your county coroner or medical examiner. Since unexplained or questionable deaths by law become "coroner's cases," she or he will be the one from whom the family seeks custody of the body. Coroner's cases may include death from violence, death when unattended by a physician, and death when in apparent good health.

Visit hospitals and senior housing facilities

Visit your local hospitals to inquire about their own policies and procedures for the release of a dead body to someone other than a licensed funeral director. Begin with the decedent affairs, patient services or patient representative offices. In some hospitals, there may be a social worker or nursing supervisor who is responsible for writing and revising policies. The purpose is not only to gather information but to gauge how a family wishing to care for its own dead might be treated. If you find that the policies are out of step with state law, offer to provide documentation and sample language to help align their policy to the law. Sample policies, tips on how to effect institutional change in health care facilities, and educational materials are available through the NHFA.

Legal Documentation

Sometimes referred to as "The Dreaded Paperwork," filing of the death certificate is really not that difficult. It usually consists of two parts. The medical portion is completed by the medical authority involved, whether that is a hospice nurse, attending physician, or Medical Examiner.

Once he or she has stated time and cause of death and signed it, the death certificate then needs to have the biographical/demographical section completed by the family. Depending on state law, a licensed funeral director or the next-of-kin acting as his or her own funeral director will sign this section.

Once complete, the death certificate must be filed within a period determined by state law. In many states, this means either presenting it in person, or to a town or city clerk or registrar in order to have it sent to Vital Statistics electronically. Some states have short forms that can be filed prior to the death certificate that expedite the process of acquiring a transport permit.

The permit for removal and transportation, which is sometimes referred to as a burial, removal and transit (BRT) permit, is usually acquired automatically after the death certificate has been successfully filed. States have their own peculiarities in terminology, but the permit is usually needed to transport the body only to the final place of disposition—the cemetery or crematory.

Some states also require a medical examiner's authorization to cremate, which may be part of the transit permit.

Check for different requirements regarding time limits for filing the final disposition paperwork, either cremation or burial, with local and/or state authorities.

Final Considerations

Preplanning pays off. If at all possible, it is wise early on to let the physician caring for the patient, the administrator of the hospital, nursing home, or hospice know of your intention to act as your own funeral director since it's impossible to know what barriers might be encountered.

If you live in a very restrictive state, you will need to enlist the aid of a cooperative funeral director. The earlier he or she is involved in the plan, the easier it will be to anticipate concerns or roadblocks.

Chapter 3
At Life's End: Support before death

By Donna Belk

In many instances the home funeral care group is a natural extension of a care group that formed not only to assist families at the time of a death and beyond but also to affirm and support them as death nears.

Families often hunger for guidance on how to help their loved one die less burdened and without unnecessary discomfort. Your community care group might want to consider creating a pamphlet with practical suggestions that family members and friends can use at life's end. Here are some tips you might want to include:

- Share memories and stories. Buy a book with blank pages, and write down family stories, recollections and thoughts. Add photos, mementos, etc., that portray the life that is passing.
- Look at family photos. Select favorites, or write stories about the photos. Add captions because once your loved one dies, no one else may be able to identify the people in the photograph.
- Put together a personal collection. This can be of recipes, poetry, stories or anything significant to the person who is dying. Add notes and record memories about the collection.
- Read. Share poetry, or read a book or magazine aloud. Discuss what stands out.
- Write. Compose a letter, or ask them to write or dictate a letter to be read to their family members in five or 10 years.
- Sing. Sing favorite family songs or lullabies, or buy an album of children's lullabies, and listen to them together. If a Threshold Choir is available in your area, consider inviting them to sing at the bedside.
- Practice visualization. Learn a simple visualization technique that you can use to help relax your loved one. This can also be used as a distraction while you wait for pain medication to bring relief.
- Practice breathing techniques. Breathing exercises may help with relaxation, which

can ease pain. They can also be useful later in the dying process when breathing can become difficult. Gently encourage them to let go of their breath and breathe deeply. Sometimes, it helps to say that you will breathe for them. Tell them how much they are loved, how much they have been loved and how safe they are.

- Bring a pet to visit. If there are no pets in the house, a visit with a well-behaved animal may be enjoyable.
- Leave the house. It can be very therapeutic to go out for a meal or short trip. This will, of course, be dependent upon the health and strength of the dying person, but anything that can be done to take the focus off the illness and put it onto something enjoyable is beneficial.
- Hold a living memorial. Invite friends and family to come over and express their love now while it can be appreciated.

Even if loved ones are unresponsive, you can still show you care. In addition to singing and reading as described above, you can:

- Provide comforting touch. Massage their hands, feet or lower legs. Rest your hand on the bed, and put their hand on top of yours.
- Whisper gentle assurances or soothing words. Repeat a comforting phrase as a sing-song while stroking their head, hand or arm. An example is, "All is well, and all is well, and all is doing very well."
- Breathe. Match your breath to the rhythm of their breath.
- Keep vigil. Sit silently by their bedside. This can be one of the most devotional acts of loving care you can offer.
- Bless or pray for them.

Purposeful Dialog

People nearing death can feel out of control, which creates more anxiety. To help them retain a sense of control, your pamphlet might also recommend ways that families can ask questions or phrase statements that encourage the involvement of the one who is dying.

In visiting the family, your community care group members can model these types of communications. When genuinely asked, questions allow the one who is dying to feel appreciated and respected and are a reminder that others know they are much more than just their illness. Here are some examples:

- If you want to tell me what kind of day you are having today, I would like to know.
- How can I help?
- I am here to support you.
- Is there something I can get for you?
- Are you feeling uncomfortable? What can we do to make you more comfortable?
- Is there anything worrying or bothering you?
- I am sorry this is happening.
- Whatever you want to do or talk about is exactly what I want to do or talk about.
- I sometimes feel I don't know what to say, so please tell me if I say the wrong thing because I only want to be helpful to you.
- We both know you are really sick. Is there anything I can do for you to ease your mind?

Life Review Questions

Life review questions are not just for soliciting reminiscences, but are also about sharing life lessons that have been learned. This reflection can bring people a sense of closure or peacefulness. If you notice any agitation by the one close to dying in asking these questions, move to a different section of questions, or wait for another time to discuss,

Parents and/or Grandparents
- What can you tell me about their lives?
- When and where were they born?
- Where did they live?
- How did they make a living?
- What were important events in their life?
- Do you recall anything important they said to you or did for you?
- What are your clearest memories of them?
- Did they have any special traditions?
- What role did each play in raising you?

Early Childhood
- What do you know about yourself as a baby?
- Were there any family stories or jokes about what you were like as a child?
- What are your earliest childhood memories?
- Do you remember any songs or lullabies?

School Years
- Do you remember the very first day?
- How did you do at school work?
- What were your relationships like with your teachers and schoolmates?
- Did you ever get into trouble? Why?
- What did you want to be when you grew up?
- Were you ever given any important advice?

Adolescence
- What can you tell me about your adolescence?
- When did you start to date?
- What were those relationships like?
- What things did you do with your friends?
- Who helped you the most in your family or outside of your family?
- What kind of jobs did you have?
- Were any very difficult or unusual?

Family Information
- Tell me about your siblings.
- Were there any conflicts in your family?
- Did your family ever move?
- What was your religious upbringing?

Adult Life
- When did you first leave home? Why?
- What's been important about your adult life?
- Tell me about your adult relationships.
- What types of jobs have you had?
- What jobs did you especially enjoy?
- What are your hobbies or other interests?
- How did you meet your spouse?
- How did you fall in love?
- When did you decide to marry?
- Was there a wedding? If so, what was it like?
- Did you have children?
- Describe your relationships with them.
- Do any family members have your traits?

Miscellaneous
- Is there anything you are very proud of?
- If you could be any age again, what age would you be? Why?
- If you could go anywhere in the world, where would it be? Why?
- What do you feel like you need to complete?
- What important messages do you want to deliver and to whom?
- Have you told everyone who needs to know how much you love them?

Chapter 4
With Our Own Hands: After-death body care

By Donna Belk

Care of the body after death engages our hearts, minds, bodies and spirits in a compassionate way and usually helps to facilitate healthy grief processes. There is no right or wrong way. You do not have to worry about hurting your loved one, and you can make this a dignified process.

If the deceased has been washed recently by caregivers, then you may choose not to wash the body. Or you may choose to do the washing regardless, simply because this is a time-honored practice and often is a source of solace to those who are grieving.

It is important to remember is that there is no hurry. Keep a quiet, slow and mindful pace. Pause from time to time to reflect on the emotional and spiritual dimensions. Offer a prayer. Take a breath. Let memories of your loved one surface. Go at your own pace.

If you initially feel uncomfortable about touching the deceased, this is not unusual. Because we have so little contact with our dead in today's society, it is normal to feel hesitant or uncomfortable at first. Just remember that this has been considered a sacred act for thousands of years and, even though dead, he or she is still our loved one. Those who do participate in body care often see their fears disappear. Like many aspects of home-based after-death care, it is a simple, practical task that might be compared to caring for an infant or bedridden patient.

Also remember that it is safe to handle a dead body. The World Health Organization, Centers for Disease Control, Center for Infectious Disease Research and Policy, and Pan American Health Organization all agree that the average dead body is neither dangerous nor contagious. Unlike a living person, the dead do not cough, spit, breathe or sweat. In the case of transmittable disease, simply take the same precautions that were used in life, such as the use of medical gloves. Ask a friend with nursing experience to help if that makes you more comfortable.

Washing and dressing of the body can be done by as few as two people, but, if possible, arrange to have up to six people on hand to help carry the body or place it into a coffin. It is usually easier to care for the body soon after death before rigor mortis has set in. Initially at the time of death the muscles relax, but within two to six hours rigor mortis begins to set in. Over time the muscles will release and the body will relax.

If you are going to have a home vigil or viewing, plan in advance where you want the body located and whether it will be laid out in a casket or on a table or bed. If practical, prepare the body in that location.

1. Gathering Supplies

It is convenient if all supplies are gathered in advance. Only gather the things that you think you will use for your situation. You may find many of these items on hand, already in the home, and do not need to be purchased.
- For washing the body: bed protector such as a shower curtain or plastic sheet to protect the mattress (if you're working on a bed), bath towels, washrags, soap, wet or dry shampoo, cotton swabs or balls, large bowl(s), rubber or latex gloves, and essential oils if desired.
- For dressing the body: final outfit or shroud/wrapping.
- For the vigil: clean bed sheets, special coverings or quilts, scarves or silk remnants, flowers, candles, religious items, family photos, decorative elements; reading lamp, chair, inspirational literature, and paper or a blank memory book.
- For cooling the body: either dry ice (using precautions) or Techni-ice can be used.
- For final disposition: purchase or make the burial or cremation container, and decorate if desired. You can purchase caskets and urns locally from craftspeople, online, or you can make your own. Arrange to rent or borrow a van, pickup truck, hearse or SUV that will accommodate the body and container.

2. Setting up the Work Space

To wash the body, have all the supplies on hand so you can work without interruption. Create enough space to comfortably move around the body. Remove medical items, supplies and as much clutter as you can to make the space feel serene.

If you have a hospital bed or a portable massage table, you will find that the height and width are more convenient and easier on your back than doing the washing in a regular bed. A sturdy folding table or other rectangular table can also be used.

3. Washing the Body

The bathing of the body can be an elaborate ritual using essential oils, prayers, candles, music or whatever is desired; or it can be a simple act of using soap and water. You can start with a ceremony, poem or prayer that feels right to you, even just a few words to set the tone. Feel the sacredness of what you are doing.

In some traditions, it is customary to wash the body as a form of ritual. You may want to create your own ritual. If so, there is no right or wrong way to do it. Let your personal preference guide you.

The bathing can take place on a bed or a table, indoors or outdoors. If prior to death the person was bathed thoroughly, no bathing or minimal bathing may be done. Rigor mortis generally sets in within the first few hours so having the body bathed and dressed soon after death is recommended.

To begin, remove the clothing and any medical devices. If the body is going to be cremated and there is a pacemaker, additional steps will need to be taken. Please see the note at the end of this chapter. Clothing can be cut off if necessary. As you work, consider using a sheet to preserve modesty as you would if the person were alive. This may also help people feel more comfortable with the process.

Before bathing, place a folded towel or disposable plastic pad under the hips and bottom, and slowly apply firm pressure just above the pubic bone to remove any urine from the bladder or bowel contents. Then remove the soiled towel or pad.

Use a gentle soap with warm water. If desired, sprinkle a few drops of essential oil and flower petals in the water. The following is a suggested order for washing the body:
- Wash the face and neck. To dry, pat the body instead of rubbing since the skin may be delicate.
- Cleanse the mouth and teeth with cotton swabs, a small rag or moisturizing sponges for the mouth. Mouthwash or diluted vinegar can be used as an antiseptic rinse to reduce odor if necessary.
- Wash the hair if desired. Dry shampoo works surprisingly well. Or use regular shampoo and water.
- Wash the arms and hands, and gently pat dry.
- Turn the body on its side. It usually takes a minimum of two people to turn the body. It is easier if you have three or four people. To turn a body onto its right side, stand on the left side of the bed (as viewed from the footboard), bend the left leg at the knee, and bring it toward the chest. Then set the left arm on top of the body. Hold the back of the bent knee and the back of the upper arm and pull toward you. Allow the body to rest against your body. Reverse the procedure to turn the body onto its left side.
- Wash the upper body front and back, and gently pat dry. Turn the body to the other side, and repeat.
- While the body is on its side, lift the upper leg a few inches so you can wash the genital area. If you are not comfortable doing this, an alternative method is to draw a washrag or towel back and forth between the legs a few times. If the deceased received a thorough bath shortly before he or she died, you may omit this step.
- Lay the body back down. Wash the legs and feet, and gently pat dry.

Before dressing, you may anoint the body with oil, fragrance or lotion as a way to bring ceremony into the process and to bless or honor the deceased.

If there are open or unsightly sores or wounds, cover them with gauze pads and seal in place with waterproof medical tape.

Although bodily discharge is not usually a problem, you may wish to place a disposable adult diaper on the body after bathing and before dressing as a preventative measure. If you are seriously concerned, you may place cotton or a tampon in the rectum to make sure any leakage is contained. You may also use cornstarch or powder in crevices if you think there is a need for it.

When finished, place a clean sheet or blanket under the body. The simplest way to do this is to roll the body to one side, roll up and push the soiled sheet against the side of the body. Then roll the body to the other side, and remove the soiled sheet. Follow the same procedure to put clean linen under the body. This sheet becomes the means by which you lift and carry the body later on, so it is important that it be sturdy and dry.

4. Additional considerations

The eyes: If you prefer the eyes be closed, it is easier to accomplish before rigor mortis occurs. Simply close the eyelids with your fingers and hold in place for a few minutes with your fingertips. Or, you can place an eye pillow or a bag of beans, rice or coins on top of the eyelids. Once rigor mortis sets in, you can remove the weights, and the eyes will usually remain closed. A dab of petroleum jelly or a small swab of cotton placed under the eyelids can also help the eyes stay closed if further action is needed.

The mouth: Thorough oral care should be done, using a toothbrush or sponge. Consider putting any dentures back in the mouth after death so the face looks more familiar to family and friends. There are several ways to close the mouth. One of the most effective ways is to use an ace bandage and loop it under the chin and secure it at the top of the head. You can also do this with a scarf. Or you can prop the jaw closed with a rolled-up hand towel fitted snugly under the chin, and place a pillow under the head. If the muscles are too stiff, massage the lower part of the jaw until it loosens enough to close the jaw. Once rigor mortis sets in, things can be removed, and the mouth will usually remain closed.

Hair washing: The hair may or may not need to be washed. Dry/no-rinse shampoo or regular shampoo with water may be used. There are excellent online resources and videos describing how this can be done if you search for "hair washing bedridden patient".

Essential areas to be washed: Skin folds and creases where skin is touching skin should be washed and dried well. You can powder with corn starch or baby powder to make sure the area stays dry. The genital and rectal areas should be washed well after pressing on the belly area before washing to help any remaining fluids be expelled. When the body is turned to the side it is easy to partially lift the deceased's leg for easy access to this area. If possible, put on an adult diaper after washing simply to prevent any mishaps or concerns that people might have about fluids leaking.

Other care: Shaving, nail care, makeup can all be done if desired, either before or after dressing the body.

Once bathing is complete, clear the area of wet items and replace with clean, dry sheets. The body can remain in place or be moved to the area where the vigil will be held, or placed in a casket, as needed.

Moving the body: Moving the body of an adult to another room or into a casket or coffin is best done with six people. With three people standing on each side, roll the sheet, which is underneath the body, so that your hands are about 3-4 inches from the body. Then everyone lifts the body together and walks in unison (shuffling steps work best) to the new location. It is a good idea to check ahead of time to make sure the body with a person on each side can fit through doors (staggering people as they go through the doorway helps). You may also want someone at the head of the body to keep the head slightly elevated. If someone has access to a body board, that can be used as an alternative.

If the body will be placed in a coffin, make sure to plan in advance how you will get it in and out of the house and how best to maneuver it through doors and up or down stairs. Go through a trial run with the coffin empty.

At this point, you may wish to take a moment of silence and say a prayer, or offer a blessing for the one who has died.

5. Dressing and Laying Out the Body for Vigil

If the body is going to be placed in a casket, dress the body first. If the body is going to be laid out on a bed or table, move the body to that location and then dress.

Rigor mortis can make dressing difficult, but limbs can be worked or massaged to remove much of the stiffness. You can be quite vigorous with the bending of the limbs; you will not harm the body.

Dress the body in whatever you deem most appropriate. A garment can be cut up the back to make it easier to put on. Undergarments, shoes and socks are not necessary, but use them if you feel it is important. If you want to shroud rather than dress the body, encircle the body in several layers of cloth, a quilt or sheets.

A body looks more natural if the head is slightly elevated. If cooling packets such as dry ice and Techni-ice are used, then the arms may need to be raised slightly by placing towels underneath them. The idea is to position the body so it appears comfortable and as natural looking as possible. If the feet fall away from one another in an unattractive way, tie a scarf around the ankles or cover the lower half of the body with a favorite quilt or scarf.

A sheer scarf can be placed over the face or any part of the body to cover anything unsightly. A scarf covering the face is a time-honored technique that conveys the message that the person is truly gone. It allows the face to be seen, but in a softer, gentler way.

Finally, place a pillow beneath the head for a more natural look, which will also help restrict fluid that may be in the stomach or lungs. You may wish to arrange the hands crossed over the heart or resting on the belly.

6. Cooling the Body

In some states cooling the body after a certain amount of time may be a legal requirement. If keeping the body at home for less than 24 hours, turning on the air conditioner or opening windows to let cold air in may suffice. However, if the vigil is to last a number of days, other means will be necessary to keep the body cool in order to slow down the process of decomposition. You can easily cool the body with Techni-ice or dry ice. Embalming is not required as more natural, less toxic alternatives are quite effective.

About Techni-Ice
- Techni-ice is a reusable ice pack that comes in flat sheets. You can order this from different suppliers and it is about $35 for 12 sheets.
- The main advantage is that you can have it on hand before you need to use it, and it is reusable by simply placing it back in the freezer. It is easy to place underneath a body because it comes in flat sheets which you can cut to just the size you need.
- To use Techni-ice you must first soak the sheets in water until they plump up, and then freeze them. When they thaw, you can simply freeze them again. The disadvantage to Techni-ice is that it thaws more easily because it is not as cold as dry ice so it will need to be replaced more often.
- Start with 6 frozen sheets of Techni-ice to cool the body. For the first 24 hours, replace them every 3-4 hours. After the first 24 hours, replace them every 8-10 hours for the remainder of the vigil.
- Remove the Techni-ice before burial if it is a green burial.

About dry ice
- Dry Ice can be purchased at many grocery stores or specialty vendors for about $1 per pound. Observe the following precautions when using dry ice:
- Never touch dry ice with bare hands; use thick gloves, a potholder or towel.
- Make sure there is good air circulation since when dry ice evaporates it emits carbon dioxide which can be dangerous to humans if not well ventilated.
- Dry ice is too cold to be cut with a knife or saw. If possible, have the dry ice company cut in 1-2" layers, otherwise smaller pieces may be created by dropping dry ice on the ground or by using a hammer to break the dry ice into smaller chunks which can then be placed in paper bags or pillowcases to make packets about the size of a paperback book.
- Start with about 30 pounds of dry ice and thereafter you will need 10-20 pounds per day.
- Place dry ice in a Styrofoam cooler since it can crack plastic containers. Do not set the cooler on wood or tile floors which can be damaged by the extreme cold of dry ice.
- Once you transfer a person to a casket if you're still using the dry ice, use a moisture barrier, such as a shower curtain, between the dry ice and casket to help reduce any condensation that may occur. If the bottom of the casket becomes wet from too much condensation it could weaken its structural integrity. Remember to remove the shower curtain before the burial if it is a green burial.

Whether using Techni-ice or dry ice bundles, put the coolant in a pillowcase or paper bag, and place under the body in these locations:
- each shoulder blade,
- the lower back and hips
- for the first few hours also place under the head and on top of the lower abdomen

An alternate method is to place sheets of Techni-ice or dry ice under the torso starting at the shoulders and extending to the lower back with one small coolant on top of the lower abdomen.

The goal is to cool off the torso and internal organs, not freeze the entire body. The skin should have a little give to it when pressed. For small bodies, such as a child, frozen gel packs may be a better option so the body does not freeze completely.

Check the coolant once or twice a day. Add more dry ice or change out the Techni-ice as needed. Be prepared to have someone help roll the body to the side when you check or replace the dry ice. Keep the head slightly elevated as you do this. Have a washcloth nearby, and protect the clothing and bedding with a towel just in case the movement causes a bit of fluid from the stomach or the lungs to exit the mouth or nose.

Twilight 2 by Ann Manning

The Art of Applying Dry Ice

By Char Barrett and Jerrigrace Lyons

How long is the family anticipating holding their home funeral vigil?

The biggest issue regarding the application of dry ice is whether families have made their final decision for a home funeral vigil. They may slowly evolve to the idea of keeping the body at home after death, during which time the body may not be cooled. They may then decide at the eleventh-hour to keep the body for another two days, and then expect dry ice to miraculously cool the body and maintain the body's current condition. By then, it's typically too late. Nature has already begun her process, and this is when families may witness purging of the body. Cooling the body within the first four to six hours following death helps to achieve a much better outcome.

Having a solid answer to this question also helps determine how much dry ice is necessary throughout the home vigil. The body will absorb the most amount of cooling from the dry ice in the first day, since the initial temperature of the body (98.6°, or often higher due to infection/tumors/etc.) is so much higher than the cool temperature required (typically 47 or 48 degrees in most states) throughout the vigil. For this reason, dry ice may or may not be used on the second day. By the third day, it is often necessary to use more, depending on whether this is the departure day for the cemetery or crematory.

How can freezing be avoided?

It's a delicate balance, and an artful one at that, managing to keep a body cool with dry ice without freezing. If potential freezing is an issue, changing out smaller amounts on a regular basis will address the issue, but the family must understand the body will need to be disturbed (moved, rolled to one side, etc.) more frequently.

Using a 3-inch foam pad on top of a mattress or massage table, or whatever surface the family chooses, helps. The foam is soft and allows the 2-inch thick (generally 7-10 lbs.) dry ice blocks to sink down somewhat so that the body remains fairly even on the surface, though an extra small pillow is usually required for the head. It also helps to protect the mattress or massage table from the freezing temperature of the dry ice (or any form of ice that may be used).

The foam pad also serves to insulate the dry ice so that it lasts longer. To further insulate and separate the ice from the body, place it in paper bags and then sandwich it between two thick bed pads or draw sheets underneath the body. Towels could also be used. It may not be necessary to change the ice that is under the body again until the third day. The ice placed on top of the body can either be smaller chunks of dry ice or Techni-ice wrapped in paper bags and towels or pillow cases. Towels help absorb moisture caused by condensation.

The ice on top is more exposed to the air and therefore will need to be changed more frequently. Dry ice on top usually needs to be changed once a day. Techni-ice needs to be changed at least twice a day and sometimes more often, depending on how warm the body is when placed there, and the temperature in the room.

Let the family know that any parts of the body nearest the dry ice will most likely freeze that part of the body. If the family is open to the use of dry ice, it certainly helps to preserve the condition of the body along with stopping any purging. With any early signs of purging or seepage of any wounds or orifices, dry ice is highly recommended, but other forms of cooling may suffice, depending on the family's preference.

Will the family have an issue with disturbing the body?

Many families choose to surround the body with elaborate sacred objects, flowers, altars, etc., and want the body minimally disturbed. In this case, the issue is a higher priority than monitoring the temperature of the body. The less dry ice you use to help avoid freezing the body, the more times you need to replace it throughout the vigil, thus disturbing the body.

Does the family have religious or spiritual objections, either to the use of dry ice or to not having the body touched at all?

Many traditional Buddhist families do not want the body touched at all, including bathing, yet understand the need to keep the body cool. Placing dry ice alongside the body, using sheets as draw cloths to avoid touching the body, is usually an effective compromise everyone can live with.

How will air temperature during the vigil influence what blankets will be used under or on top of the body?

A winter time vigil with a window slightly propped open will require less dry ice than a 90-degree summer day. Likewise, the insulating qualities of some blankets (100% wool, for example) may keep the cooling effect of the dry ice from reaching the body. Insulating the body with the right balance of blankets and "artfully applied" dry ice may keep from freezing

Many thanks to Char Barrett of A Sacred Moment and Jerrigrace Lyons of Final Passages for this content to the National Home Funeral Alliance.

7. Holding a Vigil or Visitation

If you want to hold a vigil, it can take place with the body resting on a bed, a massage table, a table or in a coffin. This is purely a matter of personal preference and convenience.

Arrange and adorn the body in a way that feels appropriate or sacred to you. If using a coffin, you can decorate it in any way you choose. If desired, put personal belongings or notes in it.

When the body is ready, prepare the room for visitors. This may include placing flowers, greenery (rosemary, for example, is the herb of remembrance), essential oil in a diffuser, candles or incense around the room. If the body is clean, there is usually no problem with odor. However, a subtle fragrance is generally a pleasant and welcoming addition to the room.

You might want to have extra chairs, a reading lamp, paper or a blank memory book with pen or pencil, music, sacred reading material and decorative items like flags on hand. It is also nice to assemble photos of the deceased and mementos of her or his life.

The manner of the viewing may be religious or secular. The vigil or visitation can occur at hours or days convenient for the family. It may be simple or elaborate to fit the personality of the deceased or the needs of the family. During a vigil, people can sit together, share silence or talk, read inspirational texts, sing, chant, invoke blessings, gently touch the body, pray, etc.

The appearance of the body may change slightly over time. Whether the vigil is 12 hours or three days, you will probably notice subtle changes such as increased paleness, the cheeks may look more sunken, rigor mortis may increase or decrease. Usually these changes are very subtle. At any point a sheer scarf may be placed over the deceased's face to help cover any changes that are unpleasant looking to the family.

8. Transporting the Body

A vehicle to transport the body to the cemetery or crematory should be arranged well in advance. You can rent or borrow a van, pickup truck or sport utility vehicle, or a funeral home can be called on to assist for a fee. (See the chapter on *Finding the Law* for required permits.)

9. Special Considerations

There may be some circumstances when a home funeral is not desired. Issues to consider include massive trauma or burns, autopsied bodies, and severe obesity, which makes turning or moving the body dangerous for caregivers. However, after a frank discussion of what to expect in these situations, it is ultimately the family's decision to make.

While rare, there are also certain infections that make a home funeral inappropriate, including septicemia, which is a virulent blood infection that produces odor and accelerates decomposition. In addition, if the deceased shows evidence of tissue gas, the body must be buried or cremated without delay. Commonly known as gangrene, the symptoms of tissue gas include strong odor and the blackening and distention of the skin. Notably, the skin "crackles" when touched. This infection spreads very quickly, and unpleasant effects can become obvious in as little as two hours. Once started, there is no way to prevent the spread of the bacteria other than the use of embalming chemicals. If it is important for the family to continue with their home funeral plans, then a funeral director should be called upon immediately to embalm. Afterward, the body may be returned home.

Note: Due to the danger of explosion, pacemakers and other internal battery-powered devices must be removed before the body is cremated. If not removed, you may be held liable for damages to the cremation chamber. Ask medical personnel to remove these devices or consult a licensed funeral director.

Peaking Out by Ann Manning

Chapter 5

Ceremony: Honoring the dying and the dead

By Kateyanne Unullisi

During a home funeral, we are challenged to blend together three powerful elements:
- Physical (where is the body going to be, are there chairs enough for people to sit down, what time does the memorial service start, etc.)
- Emotional (grieving for the loss of a person, regrets about things left undone or unsaid)
- Spiritual (bringing the mystery of life or the sacred into the space)

As a ceremonialist, funeral celebrant, and Death and Dying Guide, I have witnessed how bringing aspects of ceremony to address number three, the Spiritual element, helps bring comfort and meaning to the process of healing and connection.

When we bring intentional, sanctified ceremony and ritual into this difficult, liberating time, it can be the difference between stumbling blindly through the dark, or holding hands and moving with purpose together.

The power of ceremony and ritual is able to carry what cannot otherwise be carried, what is wordless and formless. Grief, sorrow, fear, love, loss, pain, guilt–these can be as heavy as a mountain, can be isolating and overwhelming.

There is another way. What arises in the home where death dwells is made powerful and transcendent when people choose ceremony. When people step towards death, care for their own in a natural way, and add elements of intent, and when they do this together, there is love. Healing. Gratitude. The burden is not only shared, it is lightened.

You and your family and friends are in the front of your own journey. From the vigil before the death, to all the waypoints through to death and beyond, you can create or work with others to design ceremony to help support you along the way. Use words and beliefs that are *yours*.

Below are a few ceremonies from a book that Donna Belk and I wrote together, *Home Funeral Ceremonies: A primer to honor the dying and the dead with reverence, light-heartedness and grace*. It's a small and easy-to-use book, available on Amazon. It contains these chapters that each have a few ceremony ideas for parts of a home funeral:
- Vigil before Death
- Creating Sacred Space
- Preparing the Body
- Lying in Honor
- Ending the Vigil
- At the Graveside
- Scattering Ashes
- Bridging a Death
- Recipe for Anointing Oil

Because every home funeral is unique, there may be just one or a few places to use ceremony. It's up to the people present how to approach it, and to do what is right for them. Just a simple 'let's take a moment to be present and to breathe' is a form of ceremony, bringing attention into the current moment, and uniting those present with connection.

Here are two ceremonies from the book. You can use them as written, alter them, or use them for inspiration to create your own ceremony. The 'ceremony' part is meant to be read aloud.

Do you use the word 'God'? Or does the word 'Spirit' feel more appropriate to you? Or Divine, God, Jesus, Great Spirit, The Four Directions, Love, Nature, Buddha, Grandmothers? Change the terminology, the tone, and the words as you need.

Do what feels right to you. More than anything, it matters that your ceremonies are fitting and appropriate for you, your situation, and your community.

Ceremony: Vigil before Death

A vigil and lying in honor often refer to a time when family and friends come to sit with, keep watch over, or pay their respects to a person who is dying or is deceased. Usually the dying person is sleeping or in a coma.

Use this ceremony in the time and space right before the death occurs, as a way of respecting and honoring the dying person, and the process.

It is a time of quiet reflecting and bonding with friends and others who are grieving.

Title and author of ceremony: The Great Letting Go by Kateyanne

In this short Life that only lasts an hour
How much — how little — is within our power
~ Emily Dickinson

When to use
This is the time when a person is actively dying. Caretakers and loved ones gather and wait as the dying person goes through the work of dying.

Intention
This dying process marks the beginning of a 'time out of time' period, a liminal space. Create your own intentions for blessing and releasing *<the deceased's name>*, to assist in his final letting go of the body. Keep the room quiet, gentle and soft as he would prefer. Stay clear in your intention to support the dying process, and find means to support yourselves too. This is a time of great love. It is the great letting go.

Materials needed
- Scarves to drape over harsh surfaces
- Ceremony printed out to read

Preparation
- Keep the room soft, quiet, and the light low. Turn off or remove all cell phones and items that transmit wireless energy. If there is medical equipment, do your best– perhaps cover with scarves. You will know what is right.
- Have the group gather together outside of the room, to center and to affirm their intention to support one another and to release the deceased freely. That is part one of the ceremony.
- For the second part of the ceremony, gather near to the deceased. His comfort is primary, so it is up to you and the situation if you touch, hold or cradle him. If able, everyone holding hands to create a circle would be helpful.

Part one
Centering and intention-setting, before entering the room with the dying person

We love *<the deceased's name>*. And we are grieving, dreading his death.

Perhaps our grief and dread are impeding his work of dying. Perhaps our grief and dread are keeping us from being fully present for him, for one another and for ourselves.

Let us be clear in our intention to shift these feelings, and to do it together. Let us breathe in, into our clenched and fearful hearts, the light of love. We breathe in light, into our hearts. And we breathe out fear and dread.

<Breathe in slowly. Release breath slowly>

Let us come together around *<the deceased's name>*, and share our love for him and for each other. Let us bring compassion into this moment, and acceptance, for what is happening now. We breathe in loving compassion to any place in our bodies that is shut away, is in hiding, is in pain. We breathe out the feelings of vulnerability and fear from that place.

<Breathe in slowly. Release breath slowly>

We are not ready for this. And at the same time, we are ready because there is no way around this time. We walk through it together. We are now ready to assemble at *< the deceased's name>* dying place, and mindfully say goodbye. We breathe in the light of love into our bodies, feeling into any place that does not want to release him. We breathe out our grip on him, we loosen our grip, we begin to let him move on.

<Breathe in slowly. Release breath slowly>

Mothers, Grandmothers,
all our Ancestors —
come near to us.
Bring us peace.
Fathers, Grandfathers,
all our Ancestors —
guide us, bless us,
as we draw near to you.

Part two
<At the bedside of the dying person>

We have come close to *<the deceased's name>*, to gather with one another and him as he lies dying.

<The deceased's name>, we are here to thank you, to bless you, and to release you. We love you. We will always and forever love you.

It is a lot for you to let go, to move out of your body, and to die. It is a lot for us to witness this, to hold onto our love for you, while at the same time opening to the knowing we will soon not have you with us.

We do this together, with the support and care we have for one another. We do this with you.

May the divine love of all that is surround you and help you find release. May divine love surround us as we wait with you, and bring comfort to all here in this time of the great letting go.

We are so full of gratitude for the life we have shared with you. We will miss you. We wish you easeful passage, and we will love you forever and ever.

<You could read a prayer or a poem here. And then go around the circle to individually say what each person there is grateful for and to say goodbye.>

And now there is time for each person to speak, if you choose to, and say what you have learned from *<the deceased's name>*, what you appreciate, or simply say goodbye.

We close with this invocation:

Mothers, Grandmothers,
all our Ancestors —
come near to us.
Bring us peace.
Fathers, Grandfathers,
all our Ancestors —
guide us, bless us,
as we draw near to you.

Ceremony: Creating Sacred Space

This ceremony is meant to aid in creating a space, or a sense of presence, where the heart may be spoken and heard. Perform this ceremony in the presence of the person who has died.

Title and author of ceremony: Before Preparing the Body by Donna

Our birth is but a sleep and a forgetting;
The soul that rises with us, our life's star,
Hath had elsewhere its setting
And cometh from afar;
Not in entire forgetfulness,
And not in utter nakedness,
But trailing clouds of glory do we come
From God who is our home.
~ William Wordsworth

When to use
At the start of a home funeral when people are gathered to begin with the preparations and washing of the body.

Intention
To get people working together, to acknowledge any discomfort or awkwardness there might be, and to let people know there might be mistakes made, but it is all part of the process and there is no cause for alarm or upset.

Materials needed
- No additional supplies are needed for this ceremony, although it is always more effective if the space you use is softly lit, and has beautiful items such as a vase of flowers. This helps to relax participants and brings in a feeling of the sacred.
- If you are in a space where there is medical equipment, try to remove, or cover as much of it as possible.
- Gather the supplies needed to wash the body so as soon as the ceremony concludes you can move into washing of the body.

Preparation
Quiet yourself.

Begin ceremony
We have come here today, at the start of this home funeral, to create sacred space together. Sacred space is whatever is meaningful to you, and it will act as a container or a holder for this entire event. There may be laughter, there may be tears, and these things we also include as part of our sacred space. We may fumble, drop things, or be clumsy. This, too, we include in our sacred space.

To begin our work together, our time together, let's take three harmonizing breaths together to blend our inhalations and exhalations, to act as cushions for one another, to weave together a container of respect, honor, kindness, and love on behalf of our dear one, *<the deceased's name>*.

Please inhale slowly, deeply,
<Pause>

And exhale. Sigh if you wish.

Inhale together. Exhale.

Inhale. Exhale.

Blending, sharing our breath, our intentions, harmonizing our breath, our energies, and our time together.
<Pause>

As we go about our caring for *<the deceased's name>*, remember at any time to come back to the breathing, to again establish harmony and find the balance.

I will now read a Buddhist litany for peace.

As we are together praying for Peace, let us be truly with each other.
    <Pause 3-5 seconds>
Let us pay attention to our breathing.
    <Pause 3-5 seconds>
Let us be relaxed in our bodies and our minds.
    <Pause 3-5 seconds>
Let us return to ourselves and become wholly ourselves. Let us maintain a half-smile on our faces.
    <Pause 3-5 seconds>
Let us be aware of the source of being common to us all and to all living things.
    <Pause 3-5 seconds>
Evoking the presence of the Great Compassion, let us fill our hearts with our own compassion — toward ourselves, and towards all beings, whether known to us or unknown, whether in form, or not in form.
    <Pause 3-5 seconds>
Let us be aware that we are all nourished from the same source.
    <Pause 3-5 seconds>
Let us pray that we ourselves cease to be the cause of suffering to each other.
    <Pause 3-5 seconds>
With humility and awareness, let us pray for the establishment of peace in our hearts.
    <Pause 3-5 seconds>
And within this container, of breath, of peace, of intention, we now begin our work with *<the deceased's name>*.

Healing 3 by Ann Manning

Chapter 6

Setting Out Together: What is a home funeral community care group?

By Holly Stevens

Maybe you're considering creating a home funeral community care group. Here are some examples of other community care groups.

In Dillingham, a rural community in southwestern Alaska, there is no funeral home to serve as backup. Funeral preparation involves a team of men working mostly with shovels and buckets to clear a spot amid the roots of ancient trees or on a steep slope leading to the beach. The work is backbreaking, so the diggers take turns, drinking coffee and discussing commercial fishing on their breaks. Wintertime is the most grueling; the ground yields only chips to the shovel blade, and the Alaskan winds claw at exposed skin. A "home funeral care group" here is, by necessity, the domain of weathered men, and the ceremony to honor the dead is wresting from the earth a hole big enough to accommodate the coffin.

Leaders of the Adath Jeshurun Synagogue in Minneapolis, Minnesota, found themselves alarmed at the increasing cost of funerals and the tendency of member families to depart from conservative Jewish funeral traditions. After researching Jewish laws of burial and the role of the chevra kadisha (burial society) in traditional Jewish practice, they formed their own chevra and began offering their members a plain pine box, which is provided without charge by the congregation to promote equality in final arrangements. They also negotiated arrangements with a local funeral provider that honored the requirements of their faith tradition at a reasonable cost.

In North Carolina, the Islamic Association of Raleigh recognizes Islamic burial as fard kifaya (a community affair), which exemplifies the Muslim belief that Allah is pleased with a community care group that organizes itself to bury its dead according to the teachings of the Quran. Under its leadership, the association has trained hundreds of American Muslims to wash, shroud and bury their dead, maintain Muslim cemeteries, and create funeral kits that contain appropriate shrouds for each sex as well as wooden materials for the grave. Since only men wash men and only women wash women in Islam, both the training and the response committees are organized accordingly with member duties rotating monthly through the year.

Crossings Care community care groups are forming in local communities across America, embodying the perspective of Beth Knox, founder of Crossings: Caring for Our Own at Death, who learned at the tragic death of her seven-year-old daughter, Alison, that she had the right to care for her child's body up until the moment of burial or cremation. These committees promote alternatives to conventional funeral and after-death care, forming groups of individuals who sometimes pledge to help each other care for their loved ones' remains.

The Final Affairs community care group of the Ann Arbor Friends Meeting in Michigan has hosted member forums on hospice, living wills and simple burial. This Quaker group also created a checklist to get members planning for their passing to ensure that their desires are known and to ease the logistical effort on the survivors. The checklist gathers contacts for next of kin, attorneys, insurance/financial agents, etc., as well as burial or cremation choices and requests for ceremonial songs, burial clothes and epitaphs. Some members file a copy of their checklist along with copies of their advance directives at the congregation's office.

Assessing Goals and Limitations

What are *your* home funeral community care group's aims? Here are a few guiding queries that you might consider both individually and as a group.

If your home funeral community care group functions as part of a faith community. How does home-funeral work relate to your faith community's religious beliefs, customs, values and language? To what degree is it infused with religious or spiritual motivations? The answers to these questions might lead to a compelling statement about your community care group's basic aims.

To what extent does your faith community set the pattern for acceptable funeral practices or, conversely, allow for individual choice in funeral practices? You may find clues here that define the scope of your community care group's activities. In many Catholic parishes, for instance, funeral liturgical ceremonies must be held at the church. A Catholic home funeral community care group might, therefore, focus primarily on the vigil, which can be held in the home.

Given your home funeral community care group's emphases, where does it fit most comfortably in the organizational structure of your congregation and/or its parent bodies? This, too, might influence its aims.

If your home funeral community care group is an extension of a long-standing bereavement-care group, then the primary aims likely would include offering funeral options as a healing resource for families that are hurting.

How large is your faith community? How close-knit are its members? How similar or diverse are its members' customs and perspectives when it comes to funeral options? These characteristics can help guide your community care group in establishing aims that reflect the culture of your particular community.

How committed to home funerals are the leaders of your faith community? If your faith community's guidance comes from one or two religious leaders, their perspective on home funerals may greatly influence your community care group's aims.

For any home funeral community care group, faith-based or secular. To what extent is making funerals more affordable a guiding motivation? More family centered? More environmentally responsible? More emotionally healing? More creatively expressive?

Is your home funeral community care group part of a larger organization? If so, how does your community care group relate to the parent organization's work and aims? A hospice-based home funeral community care group, for instance, might focus on expanding the role of their hospice to include the care of the dead through final disposition.

If your home funeral community care group is independent, who would benefit from its services? If it is forming as a cooperative agreement among a circle of friends who intend to support each other's families in caring for their dead, then the aims can be achieved through consensus building among its members or another agreed upon process. However, if the community care group is seeing its work primarily as influencing funeral practices in the local community, then its aims should be a response to prevailing local customs.

Once you have defined your aims as a community care group, consider the more specific activities and tasks that home funeral community care groups can assume. In the process, you will be defining the scope of your work, which will help to protect the community care group from becoming extended beyond its means. Though not a complete list of possibilities, here are some common home funeral community care group tasks to consider.

Before and during home funerals:
- Review home funeral tasks and arrange for assistance
- Assign a community care group liaison to coordinate assistance
- Assist family with practical care of the body
- Help arrange a home vigil
- Offer prayer meetings or other rituals of support for the dying as befits your community
- Maintain a home funeral supply kit
- Make or purchase a casket, shroud or cremation urn as desired
- Find a local supplier of dry ice, or stash gel packs in a convenient freezer
- Assist with purchases of dry ice or other essentials as needed
- Assist family with coordinating any visitations
- Provide a journal or register for any visitations or ceremonies
- Arrange for printed bulletins, flowers or other items for any planned ceremonies
- Recruit any pastoral ministers, musicians, pallbearers or others needed for any ceremony
- Coordinate with any licensed funeral provider that might be involved

- Arrange or provide funeral transport in keeping with state laws
- Develop a list of people to be notified immediately upon death and another for those who won't be notified until after final disposition
- Assist family in notifying friends and relatives of their loved one's death
- Maintain a list of individuals to be thanked afterward
- Gather information for the death certificate and/or obituary
- Assist family with processing death certificate and/or placing obituary
- Arrange for volunteers to answer the family's phone as needed
- Assist with caring for any children or pets in the family home
- Provide meals and/or light housekeeping for the family
- Arrange for a house sitter during publicized events to thwart would-be burglars
- Arrange for lodging and transportation of any out-of-town guests
- Follow up with the family afterward to attend to any continuing need of support

Other possible roles:
- Educate families about home funerals and other funeral options
- Provide statutory forms for advance directives, such as healthcare power of attorney, that relate to final arrangements
- Identify and proactively seek the cooperation of parties involved in arranging death certificates, obituaries and other necessary home funeral tasks
- Maintain a registry of members' final arrangement preferences
- Develop a presentation for other community care groups that might want to consider starting their own home funeral community care groups
- Record accounts of home funerals in the home funeral community care group binder

Considering the aims you have established for your home funeral community care group, what other tasks and responsibilities might you identify?

Chapter 7

Down This Path: Keep your community care group sustainable

By Holly Stevens

The effort your home funeral care group is making to define its purpose and scope no doubt will help yours be a fully functioning group. But to remain vital, your community care group will require regular tending. This chapter addresses key elements that enable home funeral care groups to remain healthy and sustainable over time.

Identify Motivations

Anyone who serves on a community care group operates from a set of motivations and assumptions that might not be fully understood—even by themselves. For some, the task element, which is what your home funeral care group formally establishes as its aims and scope, is primary; they may heartily endorse the return to less institutional forms of death care and be eager to invest their energy in making this happen in their local communities. For others, the work has a social purpose; they yearn to interact with others who share similar values and passions. For community care groups that function in a faith community, the members may see themselves as engaged in ministry or seeking spiritual growth; these groups might build into their gatherings opportunities for reflection on how the tasks at hand relate to the members' religious journeys. Others are looking to develop new skills; the home funeral care group may be a great opportunity to involve teens and young adults in a field that, so far, seems to be dominated by those on the far side of 40.

As new members join the community care group, it is wise to invite them to share something about what draws them to this work and to share with them some of the motivations of the other members. By tapping into these motivations, the community care group will identify ways to incorporate processes and experiences that mesh. For instance, a group comprised of individuals who enjoy the social aspect of their work might gather for a meal in a member's home after completing a funeral to process their shared experience.

Establish Timely Goals

Another key to sustaining a vibrant home funeral care group is to establish specific goals for each year or other selected time period. In the first year, your goals might center on training and publicity. In the second year, the focus might shift toward home funeral advocacy in the local community. Setting annual goals will help the home funeral care group pace itself and recognize that not every aim has to be fully met in the first year.

Set Times to Come Together

The home funeral care group also should determine the frequency and length of community care group meetings and responsibilities between meetings. If the community care group is part of a larger organization such as a congregation, it will also need to consider how it will report to and work with other community care groups (e.g., a nominating community care group that might regularly appoint new volunteers to the home funeral care group).

What will be the impact on the community care group if it suddenly faces several home funerals in a short period of time? How will the members build in an opportunity to reflect together on how those funerals went and to celebrate what went well? Conversely, how will the community care group remain engaged if no home funerals occur in some years?

Determine a Leadership Model

Each home funeral care group must determine the form of leadership that best serves that particular group. Some community care groups find it helpful to designate one person as the coordinator for a year or more, while others may rotate the leadership or assign leaders on an ad hoc basis. For most community care groups, it is wise to build in a process for rotating the leadership at set intervals (weekly, every two years, etc.) to avoid too much dependency on one person. If your community care group is drawn to consensus-building models, it might select a moderator whose role is to focus on group processes, look for areas of clear agreement and ensure that all members are heard while working toward a common vision. Another member might be appointed to record ideas and decisions, while yet another member might oversee logistics (speaker invitations, DVD rentals, refreshments).

Incorporate Check-In Moments

What will be the format of your continued gatherings? This book's study guide section suggests a transitional opening and closing plus experiential exercises and assignments, but ultimately your home funeral care group must decide what works best for your group. As you move beyond basic training, you might want to build into each gathering a time to go around in a circle to see what each person's focus has been in light of his or her responsibilities since the last meeting. These check-in moments can help other members identify new resources or even ward off burnout when a member expresses emerging difficulties in coping.

Reach Those You Serve

How will you publicize the community care group's services? This involves being clear about who your public is and whether it is confined only to the members of your congregation or open to any family in your town or city. Once you identify those who need to know about your community care group, brainstorm for creative ways to reach them.

Even if your funds for publicity are few, many options exist. If your home funeral care group operates within a faith community, what means does your community use to communicate (newsletters, bulletin boards, bulletins, announcements at religious gatherings, religious education classes, related community care groups, websites and member blogs)? Secular and faith-based community care groups might consider distributing news releases; writing an op-ed column for the local newsletter; asking related organizations, such as senior services entities, to publicize the community care group; sending announcements to local calendars and blogs; and hosting home-funeral-related events. You might even start your own website. In working with the news media, keep in mind that your "newness" and "uniqueness" are newsworthy. Make the most of it!

Get Organized

How will you keep records of your decisions and experiences for the benefit of others down the path? A three-ring binder can be used for the organizing of stories, plans, information and other resources. Such a record would help not only in passing along the community care group's collective wisdom to new members and leaders, but also serve as a resource for families beginning to consider their options for less institutional final arrangements.

The content in your three-ring binder will reflect your community care group's specific aims, goals and tasks. Possible items to include are:
- Our stories—accounts by funeral community care group members and the families assisted by the community care group
- Our aims—a statement reflecting the consensus of the funeral community care group members
- Our short-term goals—concrete, measurable objectives for the coming year or other time period
- Our tasks and services—the responsibilities the home funeral care group is equipped to assume as well as a statement of its scope and limitations
- Members and assigned roles—this section might include a written statement from each member about his or her experience with home funerals and motivations for being involved with the community care group
- Minutes and other records of community care group actions and decisions
- CDs containing ready-to-print PDF materials that the community care group uses repeatedly
- Forms used by the home funeral care group, such as advance directives, data to be gathered in advance for the death certificate or obituary, family funeral plans, etc.
- A registry section for the funeral plans of families to be assisted by the community care group
- Legal requirements—a place to gather statutes, letters, articles and other written material about laws affecting home funerals in your area

- Advocacy–a place to keep plans, correspondence, notes and other materials related to your community care group's work in advocating for families serving as their own funeral directors
- Publicity–a place to keep past news releases, fliers and other publicity samples as well as to maintain records of media contacts and other distribution lists
- Recommended funeral providers willing to work with family-directed funerals, including funeral homes, crematories, cemeteries, funeral transport services and gravediggers
- Liturgies, poems, meditations, music and other elements for funeral ceremonies
- Correspondence
- Checklists for funeral community care group members assisting in home funerals
- Checklists for families serving as their own funeral directors
- Literature on death, dying and after-death care and disposition rights and options
- Other media on death, dying and after-death care and disposition rights and options

Recruit New Members

How will you continually add new members to the community care group and equip them with the requisite knowledge and skills for home funeral work? Recruiting should be recognized as everyone's role and will require alertness to signs of interest in home funeral work. Often, new members will come from the families served. Some community care groups host public events to educate the community about home funerals; those who attend often become new members. Be aware, also, that some people are willing to help with specific tasks from time to time but are reluctant to participate in ongoing gatherings. What opportunities will you provide for their involvement? In a congregational setting, some churches host regular community fairs where members can sign up to serve on specific groups or task forces. If your faith community doesn't yet offer this opportunity for identifying new members, you might suggest it.

Ongoing Training

Once new members join, the best way to educate and train them is to involve them in actual home funerals. But if these events are few and far between, especially at first, consider establishing an orientation process that will equip them with basic skills and knowledge. This might include providing them with a copy of this book to read, occasionally inviting new members to come early to a gathering to watch a DVD on home funerals and hosting one or two practice body care sessions each year, for new and potential members or families.

Forge Alliances

In addition to recruiting and training new members, stay alert to opportunities to forge new alliances with like-minded organizations and individuals. Depending on your group's aims and emphasis, alliances might be sought with hospice professionals, a local chapter of Funeral Consumers Alliance (see Online Resources), a local religious leaders group, cancer support groups, funeral transport services or other freelance providers that could assist with home funerals, a sympathetic state legislator, or a motivated hospital chaplain who wants to improve protocols for releasing a body to a family acting as its own funeral director. The possibilities are endless.

Care for One Another

Finally, recognize that home funeral work, while deeply satisfying, can be fatiguing. Though members focus primarily on helping a family care for its dead, they should also care for one another. We've already suggested incorporating opportunities to reflect upon and celebrate shared funeral experiences.

Other forms of group nurture could include sending thank you notes as a member takes on or completes a significant helpful task; encouraging members to express their needs for assistance as they check in at the beginning of community care group gatherings; and occasionally breaking out of the rut to experiment with a new gathering format, time or place. Working to prevent burnout may be the greatest gift home funeral care group members can give to one another.

Looking Out by Ann Manning

How can I facilitate home funerals in my community?

From the National Home Funeral Alliance

Our movement grows because people like you have an interest and vision for your community regarding home funerals. This is still a pioneering effort in each community, and it can feel lonely. You are not alone! There's so much information and support, thanks to the early efforts of folks like yourself who work to keep this human right open to families and friends who wish for this post-death care.

Here are some ways to go about it:

1. Get educated
Become a member of the NHFA (it's free) so you can receive monthly updates and stay current with leading thoughts and recommended practices for home funerals.
Read these must-have books—written by those who know:
-*Essentials for Practicing Home Funeral Guides*
-*Home Funeral Planning Workbook for Families*

Browse articles, videos, how-to manuals, press coverage and more in the Resources section of our website.

If you want more formal training, find teachers to reach out to in your area or online.

2. Know your state laws and the issues that families face
Read "Families' Rights," and the companion piece, "What to Do When Families' Home Funeral Rights are Challenged."

Find specific laws about your state at the Funeral Ethics Organization.

Connect with your local Funeral Consumers Alliance chapter. Find a chapter in your state, talk to them, see what they have available about home funerals. If they do an annual funeral home price list survey, obtain a copy of it so you know what funeral homes are charging in your area for their various services.

3. Get to know your home funeral community
It bears repeating: become a member of the NHFA (it's free) so you can receive monthly updates and stay current with leading thoughts and recommended practices for home funerals.
Take your time and explore our website.

Follow us on Facebook for up-to-date stories, news and more.

Join us for the NHFA monthly phone conversation. This is a great place to hear other folks share their stories on what's happening in their area.

Connect with other home funeral guides and industry leaders at the NHFA conference.

4. Partner with others and cultivate conversations about home funerals
Find groups or Meetups in your area that are already discussing the topic of death and dying (such as Death Cafes).

Meet with your friends and share the idea of home funerals and see if you can answer all of their questions. The questions you *can't* answer are the important ones because they let you know where you need more information.

5. Share with others
The NHFA provides materials you may use to help teach about home funerals. You are free to print our information sheet, use our editable slide presentation, and also use our handy press packet that details how to get the word out in your community.

Write an editorial in the local paper about the

benefits of home funerals.

Get on a local radio show to talk about your experiences with home funerals.

Host a group that discusses the issues around death and dying. Perhaps there is a green cemetery in your area or interest in that to use as a starting point. Or gather friends for a study group or a book or film club.

Offer a free public talk at a library or church, or an informative lunch-and-learn to a hospice in your area.

6. As opportunities for sharing and education

develop, you can serve your community as a point or go-to person about home funerals. Create your own website. You'll find great ideas by reviewing websites that other home funeral guides have created (Just remember to respect their rights to their writing and content—be sure to create yours in your own words and style.)

Healing 2 by Ann Manning

STUDY GUIDE

Below is a suggested 10-week program for your community care group. Each session can last 1½ to 2 hours. The first two meetings would be to create the group and the structure of the group, and the following meetings would focus on the chapters in this book, with one final meeting for celebrating completion of the journey, talking about what you've learned and wrapping up loose ends.

It helps if every participant has their own copy of *Undertaken With Love* so they can make notes in the margins for their own personal use.

Session 1

Studying together

For the opening of this gathering, read the following or begin in a way that is appropriate for your group. It may be helpful to get comfortable and sit quietly for a few minutes in order to gather your thoughts and become open to sharing with others.

Ode from Recollections of Early Childhood
By William Wordsworth
Our birth is but a sleep and a forgetting:
The Soul that rises with us, our life's Star,
Hath had elsewhere its setting,
And cometh from afar:
Not in entire forgetfulness, And not in utter nakedness,
But trailing clouds of glory do we come"

Exercise
Instructions: Allow 15-20 minutes to read the introduction to *Undertaken With Love*. One person can read, or you can each take a turn reading one or two paragraphs and then passing the book along to the next person.

Discuss one or two of the questions below to help the group get to know each other and to bring awareness to some of these issues. Leave time for anyone to bring up a question for discussion.

What do you think about the idea of a home funeral in general?
*   Were there aspects to Nellie's story that you would have done differently? Or other comments about her story
*   Do you know about the legal issues in your state regarding family-directed funerals?
*   Are there memories or stories about home funerals in your family history?
*   Are there other stories to be told about funerals you have witnessed that you wish had been done differently? What specifically would you want improved or changed?
*   Ask for the meaning of a home funeral to be summarized, and if necessary, read the definition again from the introduction.

Assignment
*   Confirm the next meeting time and place
*   Read Chapter 1 ~ Then and Now: A history of home funerals

For the closing of this meeting, read the following words or end in a way that is appropriate for your group.

Elisabeth Kubler-Ross
It is not the end of the physical body that should worry us. Rather, our concern must be to live while we're alive - to release our inner selves from the spiritual death that comes with living behind a facade designed to conform to external definitions of who and what we are.

Session 2

Chapter 1 ~ Then and Now

For the opening of this gathering, read the following or begin in a way that is appropriate for your group. It may be helpful to get comfortable and sit quietly for a few minutes in order to gather your thoughts and become open to sharing with others.

A Blessing for Children
By Mark Frydenberg
May your eyes see the best in all people, May your mouth speak wisely,
May your hands reach out to others, May your feet run to do good deeds.

May you have the patience to learn, and the spirit to be playful.
May you have the will to imagine, and the freedom to dream.

May your life be long and happy, May your good name shine,
May Tradition show you The Way, May you find your place in the world.

May there be love in your heart, and a smile on your face.
May your days be filled with promise and wonder. May God grant you peace.

This poem is used with permission: Siddur Chaveirim Kol Yisraeil, Ktav Publishing House, New Jersey, 2000

Exercise
Instructions: Allow 15-20 minutes to read and ponder the following questions. Please feel free to address only the questions you feel comfortable with. You might find there are things that come up that you want to further process with a friend or counselor at a later time.

Afterward, discuss one or two of the questions to help the group get to know each other and to bring awareness to some of these issues. Leave time for anyone to bring up a question of particular impact for discussion.

Death Questionnaire
Think of when you had a significant experience with death.
- How well did you know the person that died?
- What was your experience in being with someone when they were dying?
- When you were first told of the death, how did you feel?
- What was it that most helped you deal with the death?
- What was it that most hindered you in dealing with the death?
- What was of most support to you in dealing with the death?
- What was the most confusing part of dealing with this death?
- What was the hardest part of dealing with this death?
- What do you remember most vividly about how this death affected you and those around you?
- Dealing with death can be difficult, but is there anything that happened for which you are grateful?

- If you have experience in being with someone when they were dying, what advice could you offer to others in that same situation?
- What one thing impressed you as an important part of the whole death process?
- Looking back, what do you think about the way the medical community handled the situation?
- If hospice was involved, what did you feel about your contact with them during this experience?
- Looking back on what you went through with the funeral and the people in attendance, what stands out most about the funeral?
- If you were to be able to have one last conversation with your deceased loved one, what might you say to him or her? What might he or she say to you?

Assignment
Read Chapter 2 ~ Finding the Law: Are home funerals legal?

For the closing of this meeting, read the following poem or end in a way that is appropriate for your group.

Gone from my sight

I am standing on the seashore. A ship at my side spreads her white sails to the morning breeze and starts for the blue ocean. She is an object of beauty and strength, and I stand and watch her until at length, she is a speck of white cloud just where the sea and sky come to mingle with each other.

Then someone at my side says, "There! She's gone!" Gone where? Gone from my sight, that is all. She is just as large in mast and hull and spar as she was when she left my side, and she is just as able to bear her load of living weight to her destined harbor.

Her diminished size is in me, not in her. And just at the moment when someone at my side says, "There! She's gone!" There are other voices ready to take up the glad shout, "Here she comes!" And that is dying.

This poem is usually credited to Henry Van Dyke (1852-1933) or Bishop Charles Henry Brent (1862-1926).

Session 3

Chapter 2 ~ Finding the Law

For the opening of this gathering, read the following or begin in a way that is appropriate for your group. It may be helpful to get comfortable and sit quietly for a few minutes in order to gather your thoughts and become open to sharing with others.

The Book of the Dead
Egyptian prayer c. 4500 B.C.
As each day ends, may I have lived That I may truly say:
I did no harm to human kind, From truth I did not stray;
I did no wrong with knowing mind, From evil I did keep;
I turned no hungry person away, I caused no one to weep.

Exercise
Share and discuss: Fran Miner, an Episcopalian in Billings, Montana, handled everything herself when her mother died in 1995. It was not an easy process. All along the way, people questioned whether she was allowed to do it.

The nursing home said she couldn't move the body. "The funeral people said I couldn't do it." Even the coroner's office, at first, said "Forget it." The County Records Office refused her a death certificate.

"I called back the coroner's office, and a different man said, 'Sure you can do it,'" and helped her. He then said the same to the nursing home and the county offices who gave her the blank death certificate to have filled out. Finally, Miner and her sons were able to transport her mother to the crematory in a cardboard box that Miner lined and decorated herself with pink satin.

"I beat the system, and I took care of my mother... I stood up to everybody ... I was so determined to do this," said Miner, who had spent the last days holding and singing to her mother and wanted to finish her task. (Nan Cobbey, *Episcopal Life*, March 2000)

Role play: Take turns role playing as a person making the above requests to a government or care facility worker. The person playing the worker will draw out of a hat one of three scenarios: The worker will refuse to give the information; the worker will give the information willingly; or the worker will only give it unwillingly. Afterward, brainstorm for methods you can employ to invite a worker to want to help you succeed.

Assignment
- Read Chapter 3 ~ At Life's End: Support before death
- Using the methods described in the "Finding the Law" chapter, search for your state's laws and hospital policies.

For the closing of this meeting, read the following expression or end in a way that is appropriate for your group.

American Indian expression
When you were born, you cried and the world rejoiced.
Then live your life in such a way that when you die, nothing is remiss
and the world will cry whilst you feel bliss.

Session 4

Chapter 3 ~ At Life's End

For the opening of this gathering, read the following or begin in a way that is appropriate for your group. It may be helpful to get comfortable and sit quietly for a few minutes in order to gather your thoughts and become open to sharing with others.

A psalm of David
Psalm 139: 7-10
Whither shall I go from thy Spirit?
Or whither shall I flee from thy presence? If I ascend up into heaven, thou art there:
If I make my bed in hell, behold, thou art there. If I take the wings of the morning,
and dwell in the uttermost parts of the sea, Even there shall thy hand lead me,
and thy right hand shall hold me.

Exercise
Total time: 35 minutes
Instructions: Pair off in groups of three. Take 5 minutes to read the instructions below. In 10-minute sessions, two members of the group will ask questions of the third member. The questions can be in any order. When the 10 minutes are up, switch roles until each member of the group has been interviewed.

Life Review
The purpose of a life review is to be able to paint a picture or tell the story of the person being interviewed. You are not trying to gather a collection of facts so much as the person's story. Avoid letting the interview become a question-and-answer session. Instead, strive for a flowing conversation. Begin by saying: "I'd like to find out about your life history. Could you tell me about it? Tell me as if you were telling me the story your life." Where they start their story and how they tell it will reveal what immediately strikes them as important.

Most people will skip over many details. If the details seem important, use open-ended questions to encourage more sharing of information. For example: And then what happened? What did you do after that? How did you feel about that?

Another technique to encourage a person to go into more detail is to mirror back something important about what they've just said. You can repeat the exact words, or you can paraphrase. You can even add a thought you had or a feeling you sensed in something they said. For example:
> *Interviewee:* My mother taught me to sew. It was one of the times I felt closest to her.
> *Interviewer:* It seems like you enjoyed being close to your mother.

Other examples of mirroring are:
> I guess you really enjoyed that time of your life. It sounds like it upset you when she said that. It seems like that was an important event.

Try to talk in whatever way seems to be the preference of the person being interviewed. Pay careful attention to how the person is responding to your questions, and always be respectful of his or her privacy. If the person is uncomfortable discussing some aspect of his or her life, don't press for an answer. Simply move on.

When used in real end-of-life scenarios, avoid feeling the need to be constantly upbeat when the situation may be quite the opposite. And remember that sometimes words are not needed; just sitting together in silence can be sacred. Take your cues from the person who is near death. Avoid telling your own story. Place his or her needs at the heart of the matter.

An extensive list of potential life review questions may be found at the end of this chapter.

Assignment
- Read Chapter 4 ~ With Our Own Hands: After-death body care.
- Interview elderly friends or relatives who have memories of funerals that took place in the home when they were young. Record their story to share at the next meeting. Alternatively, find written accounts of home funerals.
- Coordinate and gather supplies in advance to hold a practice body preparation during the next session.

For the closing of this gathering, recite the following responsive reading or end in a way that is appropriate for your group.

Form a circle. Then, going in a clockwise direction, let each member take turns reading one line, while the group responds with the refrain.

Blessed Are These Hands
By Holly Stevens
Says one: Blessed are these hands that have held an infant.
Refrain: Blessed are our lives, and blessed our hands with which we serve.

Says one: Blessed are these hands that have closed a casket.
Refrain: Blessed are our lives, and blessed our hands with which we serve.

Says One: Blessed are these hands that have carved and painted.
Refrain: Blessed are our lives, and blessed our hands with which we serve.

Says One: Blessed are these hands that have worn thin with use.
Refrain: Blessed are our lives, and blessed our hands with which we serve.

Says One: Blessed are these hands that have brushed away tears.
Refrain: Blessed are our lives, and blessed our hands with which we serve.

Says One: Blessed are these hands that have turned pages of ancient texts.
Refrain: Blessed are our lives, and blessed our hands with which we serve.

Says One: Blessed are these hands that have scripted a letter to a lonesome friend.
Refrain: Blessed are our lives, and blessed our hands with which we serve.

Says One: Blessed are these handsthat have been held back in anger.
Refrain: Blessed are our lives, and blessed our hands with which we serve.

Says One: Blessed are these hands that have prepared a nourishing meal.
Refrain: Blessed are our lives, and blessed our hands with which we serve.

Says One: Blessed are these hands that have been raised in praise.
Refrain: Blessed are our lives, and blessed our hands with which we serve.

Says One: Blessed are these hands we now join in love.
Refrain: Blessed are our lives, and blessed our hands with which we serve.

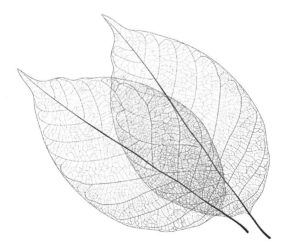

Session 5

Chapter 4 ~ With Our Own Hands

For the opening of this gathering, read the following or begin in a way that is appropriate for your group. It may be helpful to get comfortable and sit quietly for a few minutes in order to gather your thoughts and become open to sharing with others.

Deep Peace
(excerpts from an old Gaelic blessing)
Deep peace I breathe into you … Deep peace, a soft white dove to you; Deep peace, a quiet rain to you; Deep peace, an ebbing wave to you!
Deep peace, red wind of the east from you; Deep peace, grey wind of the west to you; Deep peace, dark wind of the north from you; Deep peace, blue wind of the south to you!
Deep peace, pure red of the flame to you; Deep peace, pure white of the moon to you; Deep peace, pure green of the grass to you; Deep peace, pure brown of the earth to you; Deep peace, pure grey of the dew to you, Deep peace, pure blue of the sky to you!
Deep peace of the running wave to you, Deep peace of the flowing air to you, Deep peace of the quiet earth to you … Peace, Deep Peace!

Exercise
Coordinate and gather supplies in advance to hold a mock body preparation. In this practice session include moving the body from one place to another, and include carrying the body through a doorway. After this session discuss what could have been done more efficiently, and what emotions came up for people.

Assignment
- Read Chapter 5 ~ Ceremony: Honoring the dead and the dying
- As an individual, write down what you might consider to be the basic aim of your community care group. Which tasks would you associate with this aim? Which tasks would you consider to fall outside the scope of your aim?
- Come to the next gathering with the dual intention of offering your perspectives on aim and scope as well as holding back from doggedly imposing your preferences on the whole community care group if no easy consensus can be reached.

For the closing of this meeting, read the following blessing or end in a way that is appropriate for your group.

Cherokee Prayer Blessing
May the warm winds of heaven blow softly upon your house.
May the Great Spirit bless all who enter there. May your moccasins make happy tracks in many snows,
and may the rainbow always touch your shoulder.

Session 6

Chapter 5 ~ Ceremony

For the opening of this gathering, read the following or begin in a way that is appropriate for your group. It may be helpful to get comfortable and sit quietly for a few minutes in order to gather your thoughts and become open to sharing with others.

Prayer of Faith
Author Unknown
We trust that beyond absence there is a presence.
That beyond the pain there can be healing.
That beyond the brokenness there can be wholeness.
That beyond the anger there may be peace.
That beyond the hurting there may be forgiveness.
That beyond the silence there may be the word.
That beyond the word there may be understanding.
That through understanding there is love.

Exercise
Divide into groups of three and come up with scenario that you will create a short ceremony for. Make sure one group is a ceremony before death, one during body care, and one for vigil. Consult the book if your group owns a copy.

Assignment
- Read Chapter 6 ~ *Setting Out Together: What is a home funeral committee care group?*
- As an individual, write down what you might consider to be the basic aim of your community care group. Which tasks would you associate with this aim? Which tasks would you consider to fall outside the scope of your aim?
- Come to the next gathering with the dual intention of offering your perspectives on aim and scope as well as holding back from doggedly imposing your preferences on the whole community care group if no easy consensus can be reached.

For the closing of this gathering, read the following blessing or end in a way that is appropriate for your group.

A Cornish blessing
I lay my head to rest
and in doing so
lay at your feet
the faces I have seen, the voices I have heard, the words I have spoken
the hands I have shaken, the service I have given, the joys I have shared, the sorrows revealed.
I lay them at your feet
and in doing so
lay my head to rest

Session 7

Chapter 6 ~ Setting Out Together

For the opening of this gathering, read the following or begin in a way that is appropriate for your group. It may be helpful to get comfortable and sit quietly for a few minutes in order to gather your thoughts and become open to sharing with others.

We Give Thee but Thine Own
By William Walham How, 1864
We give Thee but Thine own, Whate'er the gift may be;
All that we have is Thine alone, A trust, O Lord, from Thee.
May we Thy bounties thus As stewards true receive,
And gladly, as Thou blessest us, To Thee our first fruits give.
To comfort and to bless, To find a balm for woe,
To tend the lone and fatherless Is angels' work below.

Exercise
Using the main text for this chapter, consider the aims that each member identified in preparation for the gathering. Assign one member to record the aims suggested. Where are the commonalities? Where are the convergences? In a similar process, consider the limitations that the group intends to place on its scope.

Finally, use the checklist in the text to identify tasks that relate to the agreed upon aims. Brainstorm additional tasks that might not be listed but would be central to the community care group's aims. Have you been careful to consider your limitations, as well?

Assignment
- Read Chapter 7 ~ Down This Path: Keep your community care group sustainable.
- If the community care group has reached consensus on its aims and limitations, assign one member to write an announcement of the community care group's formation and purpose that can be considered at the next gathering.
- Ask another member to purchase for the next gathering (and perhaps design an inviting cover for) a 3-ring binder to serve as the community care group's receptacle for stories, information, plans and other resources.
- Invite all members to brainstorm ways that the home funeral care group can make its presence known and publicize its services. Come prepared to develop a publicity plan at the next gathering.

For the closing of this gathering, create the following group poem or end in a way that is appropriate for your group.

Have each member silently identify one or two loved ones who have passed and some small specific memory that brings them joy to recall—something that can be shared in one sentence.

As an example:

Miriam, I remember you holding apples in both hands.
Daddy, I remember you recording Central Park sounds on reel-to-reel tapes.

Light a candle as members reflect. Then invite members to share their poem fragments one at a time in clockwise order, forming a group poem, to honor the ones who have crossed.

Sessions 8 and 9

Chapter 7 ~ Down This Path

For the opening of this gathering, read the following or begin in a way that is appropriate for your group. It may be helpful to get comfortable and sit quietly for a few minutes in order to gather your thoughts and become open to sharing with others.

There is a Spirit
by James Naylor. 17th century Quaker martyr
Can I, imprisoned, body-bounded, touch the starry robe of God, and from my soul
my tiny Part, reach forth to this great Whole and spread my Little to the infinite Much, When Truth
forever slips from out my clutch, and what I take indeed, I do but dole
in cupfuls from a rimless ocean-bowl
that holds a million million million such?
And yet, some Thing that moves among the stars, and holds the cosmos in a web of law,
moves too in me: a hunger, a quick thaw of soul that liquefies the ancient bars,
as I, a member of creation, sing
the burning oneness binding everything.

Exercise
- Have members participate in a check-in time to share what they've done since the last gathering.
- If needed, continue working on aims and scope.
- Begin defining short-term goals.
- Decide frequency and content of upcoming meetings.
- Decide who will lead the meetings.
- Assess the meeting format you're using. Does it need to change?
- Brainstorm contents for the home funeral binder. Assign parts.
- Brainstorm how to publicize the home funeral community care group.
- Assign roles.

Assignment
- The aims and goals your home funeral care group establishes, as well as your schedule for future gatherings of the community care group, will determine any assignments to be made.
- For part 2 of this topic, or Session 9, ask for volunteers to bring an opening and closing piece to read at the next meeting.

For the closing of this gathering, read the following psalm or end in a way that is appropriate for your group.

Psalm 23: A psalm of David
The Lord is my shepherd; I shall not want.
He maketh me to lie down in green pastures: he leadeth me beside the still waters.
He restoreth my soul: he leadeth me in the paths of righteousness for his name's sake.
Yea, though I walk through the valley of the shadow of death, I will fear no evil: for thou art with me;
thy rod and thy staff they comfort me.

Thou preparest a table before me in the presence of mine enemies: thou anointest my head with oil; my cup runneth over.

Surely goodness and mercy shall follow me all the days of my life: and I will dwell in the house of the Lord for ever.

Session 10

Decide how you will celebrate completing this 10-week course. Here are some ideas

- Invite others to join in on your last meeting and summarize what was covered in the course.
- Allow each participant an opportunity to say what they got out of the course, and if it has changed them in some way.
- Issue *Certificates of Completion* to all participants.
- Discuss the next steps, if any, for your group.
- Celebrate in your own way.

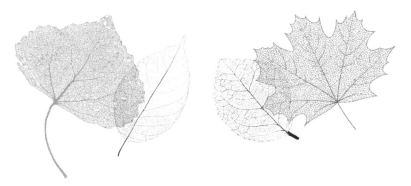

Online Resources

The National Home Funeral Alliance, www.homefuneralalliance.org
An educational nonprofit whose mission is to educate and empower families to care for their own after death.

The Centre for Natural Burial, www.naturalburial.coop
A resource center for green burial information and products, including a green cemetery locator.

Federal Trade Commission, www.ftc.gov/bcp/rulemaking/funeral/index.shtm
A resource for Funeral Rule information, consumer literature, industry compliance guidelines and the registration of complaints.

Funeral Consumers Alliance (FCA), www.funerals.org
A nonprofit organization dedicated to protecting the rights of funeral consumers. FCA has approximately 100 state chapters. Online forums and a discussion group are available.

Funeral Ethics Organization, www.funeralethics.org
Founded by Lisa Carlson to promote ethical dealings in all death-related transactions.

Green Burial Council, www.greenburialcouncil.org
Founded by Joe Sehee, the council establishes standards and provides certification for green cemeteries.

Natural Death Center, www.naturaldeath.org.uk
A UK-based organization providing advice on and support of family-organized funerals and natural burial grounds.

National Home Funeral Alliance books

- *Home Funeral Planning Workbook for Families*
  Taking care of after-death details can be an overwhelming experience for families in grief. Use the checklist and suggestions to help a family make all the decisions needed for a home funeral.
- *Essentials for Practicing Home Funeral Guides* is a resource guide for people who are offering Home Funeral Guide services. It contains documents for use by both the family and the Home Funeral Guide which help to define and clarify the tasks that will be carried out by the home funeral guide, as well as tasks for the family. It is a manual, template, and best practices all-in-one collection that every home funeral guide needs to organize necessary paperwork in order to ensure consistent, quality service to families caring for their own after death.
- *Building Bridges along the Death Care Continuum* is a book advocating for home funerals in hospices, hospitals, and care facilities.
- *Undertaken With Love*
  A home funeral guidebook for families and community care groups.

Made in the USA
Las Vegas, NV
31 December 2021